PRIDE

The other side of money.

NOTE: ALL SCRIPTURES ARE QUOTED FROM
www.biblegateway.com

TABLE OF CONTENTS

INTRODUCTION

Money has been put in the same category with God. Satan is not mentioned to be contending with God but money is.

Matthew 6:24
No one can serve two masters. Either you will hate the one and love the other, or you will be devoted to the one and despise the other. You cannot serve both God and money.

Money has proven to do what God can do, actually, it's said to be an answer to all things.

Ecclesiastes 10:19
money answereth all things.

The place of money is undeniable. The power money has is evident. Religion may try to act like all we need is God but that lie doesn't stand for a long time. Time proves that those religious people need money also.
Most people appear humble but wait until money gets in their hands then their true nature will manifest. All around money is exalted that every person is in a hurry to get it.

Matthew 6:25-34

Therefore I tell you, do not worry about your life, what you will eat or drink; or about your body, what you will wear. Isn't life more than food, and the body more than clothes? Look at the birds of the air; they do not sow or reap or store away in barns, and yet your heavenly Father feeds them. Are you not much more valuable than they? Can any one of you by worrying add a single hour to your life?

"And why do you worry about clothes? See how the flowers of the field grow. They do not labour or spin. Yet I tell you that not even Solomon in all his splendour was dressed like one of these. If that is how God clothes the grass of the field, which is here today and tomorrow is thrown into the fire, will he not much more clothe you—you of little faith? **So do not worry, saying, 'What shall we eat?' or 'What shall we drink?' or 'What shall we wear?'** *For the pagans run after all these things,* **and your heavenly Father knows that you need them.** But seek first his kingdom and his righteousness, and all these things will be given to you as well. Therefore do not worry about tomorrow, for tomorrow will worry about itself. Each day has enough trouble of its own.

The world shows the beauty money brings, preachers now have money as their main topics, the force of money is so strong and the earlier you embrace that the better.

1st John 2:15-17
Do not love the world or anything in the world. If anyone loves the world, love for the Father is not in them. For everything in the world—the lust of the flesh, the lust of the eyes, and the pride of life—comes not from the Father but from the world. The world and its desires pass away, but whoever does the will of God lives forever.

The agenda of my writing is not to magnify money but to bring a balance between God and money. I desire to show you that if you don't set your heart right with God first, the power of money will turn you against God.

Both money and God are after your heart, the choice is yours. The one you choose will be your treasure and your heart will be there.

Matthew 6:19-21

Do not store up for yourselves treasures on earth, where moths and vermin destroy, and where thieves break in and steal. But store up for yourselves treasures in heaven, where moths and vermin do not destroy, and where thieves do not break in and steal. **For where your treasure is, there your heart will be also.**

Money by itself is not evil for it is just a tool of exchange, the spirit behind it is mammon which will enslave you all the days of your life if you don't let God have his proper place. The moment your heart is removed from God, the love of money will creep in and someone can do anything to get it even if it means killing or stealing.

James 4:1-7

What causes fights and quarrels among you? Don't they come from your desires that battle within you? You desire but do not have, so you kill. You covet but you cannot get what you want, so you quarrel and fight. You do not have because you do not ask God. When you ask, you do not receive, because you ask with wrong motives, that you may spend what you get on your pleasures.

You adulterous people, don't you know that friendship with the world means enmity against God? Therefore, anyone who chooses to be a friend of the world becomes an enemy of God. Or do you think Scripture says without reason that he jealously longs for the spirit he has caused to dwell in us? But he gives us more grace. That is why Scripture says:

"God opposes the proud
    but shows favour to the humble."
 Submit yourselves, then, to God. Resist the devil, and he will flee from you.

Stay with God and he will ensure all you need finds you for he is your provider.

Psalms 23:1
The Lord is my shepherd, I lack nothing.

Philippians 4:19
And my God will meet all your needs according to the riches of his glory in Christ Jesus.

Judas was a disciple of Jesus, his heart however was not with him. Judas' heart had been shifted from God to money and he was willing to steal and even to betray Jesus just for money.

John 12:1-8
Six days before the Passover, Jesus came to Bethany, where Lazarus lived, whom Jesus had raised from the dead.Here a dinner was given in Jesus' honour. Martha served, while Lazarus was among those reclining at the table with him. **Then Mary took about a pint of pure nard, an expensive perfume; she poured it on Jesus' feet and wiped his feet with her hair.** And the house was filled with the fragrance of the perfume.

But one of his disciples, Judas Iscariot, who was later to betray him, objected, "Why wasn't this perfume sold and the money given to the poor? It was worth a year's wages." He did not say this because he cared about the poor but because he was a thief; as keeper of the money bag, he used to help himself to what was put into it.

"Leave her alone," Jesus replied. "It was intended that she should save this perfume for the day of my burial. You will always have the poor among you,but you will not always have me."

Matthew 26:14-16
Then one of the Twelve—the one called Judas Iscariot—went to the chief priests and asked, "What are you willing to give me if I deliver him over to you?" So they counted out for him thirty pieces of silver. From then on Judas watched for an opportunity to hand him over.

It didn't end well with Judas for he ended up taking his own life.

Mathew 27:3-5
Judas saw that they had decided to kill Jesus. He was the one who had handed him over. When he saw what happened, he was very sorry for what he had done. So he took the 30 silver coins back to the priests and the older leaders. Judas said, "I sinned. I handed over to you an innocent man to be killed."
The Jewish leaders answered, "We don't care! That's a problem for you, not us."
So Judas threw the money into the Temple. Then he went out from there and hanged himself.

The desire to get money can be strong in life that people can use God and others to get money.
Find people so committed to God, the church, their marriages, families etc until money gets in their hands then they become someone else.

1st Timothy 6:6-10
But godliness with contentment is great gain.For we brought nothing into the world, and we can take nothing out of it. But if we have food and clothing, we will be content with that. Those who want to get rich fall into temptation and a trap and into many foolish and harmful desires that plunge people into ruin and destruction. For the love of money is a root of all kinds of evil. Some people, eager for money, have wandered from the faith and pierced themselves with many griefs.

Don't blame them, their hearts were not anchored in the right place.
It's a journey to shift your heart from the love of money to love God so much that the presence of money don't change anything.
I know someone is saying,"I can't leave God for money" yes you can!
Satan will use the confidence money gives to show you God is of no value in your life after all what God could do money can now do.

Hebrews 6:19
We have this hope as an anchor for the soul, firm and secure. It enters the inner sanctuary behind the curtain.

Jeremiah 17:1-10
This is what the Lord says:

"**Cursed** is the one who trusts in man,
  who draws strength from mere flesh
  and **whose heart turns away from the Lord.**
That person will be like a bush in the wastelands;
  they will not see prosperity when it comes.
They will dwell in the parched places of the desert,
  in a salt land where no one lives.

"**But blessed is the one who trusts in the Lord,
  whose confidence is in him.**
They will be like a tree planted by the water
  that sends out its roots by the stream.
It does not fear when heat comes;
  its leaves are always green.
It has no worries in a year of drought
  and never fails to bear fruit."
The heart is deceitful above all things
  and beyond cure.
  Who can understand it?
"I the Lord search the heart
  and examine the mind,
to reward each person according to their conduct,
  according to what their deeds deserve."

Independence is the agenda of satan and he will ensure you do everything to get money so that finally you can break free from the authority of God.

That will not be the beginning of freedom but the start of another form of slavery. From the slavery of poverty to the slavery of money.

However, if you let your heart be surrendered to God fully, no matter the amount of money you will get, you will still be submitted to God and experience real freedom.

Poverty is bad and we should fight it with all we have. However, be careful not to fall into the trap Satan puts on the other side, of being a slave of the spirit of mammon. Lack of money is defined as poverty and the presence of money if not careful brings pride(the feeling that you nolonger need God).

The only person God has declared to be an enemy to is a proud person. For pride brings confidence in something or someone else other than God.

1st peter 5:6
   Likewise you younger people, submit yourselves to your elders. Yes, all of you be submissive to one another, and be clothed with humility, for

"God resists the proud,
But gives grace to the humble."

Therefore humble yourselves under the mighty hand of God, that He may exalt you in due time.

CHAPTER ONE: SATAN

Satan, also known as the devil, had been the fallen angel associated with the evil in the world. God didn't create him as Satan for he is a good God and all he creates is good. God created him as lucifer. Set him above all angels and made him so beautiful, well equipped as the angel in charge of worship. At that time he was submitted to God's authority. He was humble, the thing that makes God lift someone by adding his grace. God exalted Lucifer and he reached a point and saw he could take the position of God. His heart was moved from obeying, submitting to God's authority and depending on God's grace to believing he could live without God.

Pride set in Lucifer's heart and he felt he didn't need God. That led him to influence some angels in heaven to be on his side and turn against God.

Everything God created was for his pleasure. When lucifer decided not to be part of that purpose but to bring plesure to himself, he fell from his rightful position.

He was in charge of worship, he saw God being worshipped and he desired to be worshipped instead of worshipping.

That's when war broke in heaven for out of that desire to be independent from God he became satan/devil/old serpent/dragon.

Psalms 136:1
Give thanks to the Lord, for he is good.
 For his mercy endures forever.

Isaiah 14:12-15
How you are fallen from heaven,
O Lucifer, son of the morning!
How you are cut down to the ground,
You who weakened the nations!
For you have said in your heart:
'I will ascend into heaven,
I will exalt my throne above the stars of God;
I will also sit on the mount of the congregation
On the farthest sides of the north;
 I will ascend above the heights of the clouds,
I will be like the Most High.'
 Yet you shall be brought down to Sheol,
To the lowest depths of the Pit.

Ezekiel 28:12-17
Thus says the Lord God:
"You were the seal of perfection,

Full of wisdom and perfect in beauty.
You were in Eden, the garden of God;
Every precious stone was your covering:
The sardius, topaz, and diamond,
Beryl, onyx, and jasper,
Sapphire, turquoise, and emerald with gold.
The workmanship of your timbrels and pipes
Was prepared for you on the day you were created.
"You were the anointed cherub who covers;
I established you;
You were on the holy mountain of God;
You walked back and forth in the midst of fiery stones.
You were perfect in your ways from the day you were created,
Till iniquity was found in you.
"By the abundance of your trading
You became filled with violence within,
And you sinned;
Therefore I cast you as a profane thing
Out of the mountain of God;
And I destroyed you, O covering cherub,
From the midst of the fiery stones.
"**Your heart was lifted up because of your beauty;**
You corrupted your wisdom for the sake of your splendour;
I cast you to the ground,
I laid you before kings,
That they might gaze at you.

Revelation 12:7-9
Then war broke out in heaven. Michael and his angels fought against the dragon, and the dragon and his angels fought back. But he was not strong enough, and **they lost their place in heaven. The great dragon was hurled down—that ancient serpent called the devil, or Satan,**

who leads the whole world astray. He was hurled to the earth, and his angels with him.

Pride leads to a fall not exaltation. Independence from God's authority and ways leads to fall from his grace/strength/help. This is the trap many fall into the planner being satan. He will find a strong area in your life and make you think you don't need God for you have it. Be careful.

Proverbs 16:18
Pride goeth before destruction, and an haughty spirit before a fall.

Deuteronomy 8:12-18
when you eat and are satisfied, when you build fine houses and settle down, and when your herds and flocks grow large and your silver and gold increase and all you have is multiplied, then **your heart will become proud and you will forget the Lord your God,** who brought you out of Egypt, out of the land of slavery. He led you through the vast and dreadful wilderness, that thirsty and waterless land, with its venomous snakes and scorpions. He brought you water out of hard rock. He gave you manna to eat in the wilderness, something your ancestors had never known, to humble and test you so that in the end it might go well with you. You may say to yourself, "My power and the strength of my hands have produced this wealth for me." But **remember the Lord your God, for it is he who gives you the ability to produce wealth,** and so confirms his covenant, which he swore to your ancestors, as it is today.

When God came on earth, that evil desire to be worshipped was still in Satan's heart. He asked the son of God to bow and worship him and he would give him all things. But

Jesus' heart was on God and his worship and loyalty belonged to him only.

Luke 4:5-8
The devil led him up to a high place and showed him in an instant all the kingdoms of the world. And he said to him, "I will give you all their authority and splendour; it has been given to me, and I can give it to anyone I want to. If you worship me, it will all be yours."
Jesus answered, "It is written: 'Worship the Lord your God and serve him only.'

Today, you will have to make the same choice between who you will serve; God or satan.

John 4:23-24
Yet a time is coming and has now come when the true worshipers will worship the Father in the Spirit and in truth, for they are the kind of worshipers the Father seeks. God is spirit, and his worshipers must worship in the Spirit and in truth."

Deuteronomy 30:15-20
See, I set before you today life and prosperity, death and destruction. For I command you today to love the Lord your God, to walk in obedience to him, and to keep his commands, decrees and laws; then you will live and increase, and the Lord your God will bless you in the land you are entering to possess.
But if your heart turns away and you are not obedient, and if you are drawn away to bow down to other gods and worship them, I declare to you this day that you will certainly be destroyed. You will not live long in the land you are crossing the Jordan to enter and possess.

This day I call the heavens and the earth as witnesses against you that **I have set before you life and death, blessings and curses. Now choose life, so that you and your children may live** and that you may love the Lord your God, listen to his voice, and hold fast to him. For the Lord is your life, and he will give you many years in the land he swore to give to your fathers, Abraham, Isaac and Jacob.

CHAPTER TWO: ADAM

When satan fell from heaven to earth, him and his demons destroyed all that God had made. God recreated everything and created Adam to be in charge. He gave Adam all things only the tree of good and evil he was not to eat from.
God created a woman for Adam and he taught Eve God's instructions.

Genesis 1:1-5

In the beginning God created the heavens and the earth. Now the earth was formless and empty, darkness was over the surface of the deep, and the Spirit of God was hovering over the waters.
And God said, "Let there be light," and there was light. God saw that the light was good, and he separated the light from the darkness. God called the light "day," and the darkness he called "night." And there was evening, and there was morning—the first day.

Genesis 1:26-27

Then God said, "Let us make mankind in our image, in our likeness, so that they may rule over the fish in the sea and the birds in the sky, over the livestock and all the wild animals, and over all the creatures that move along the ground."

So God created mankind in his own image,
in the image of God he created them;
male and female he created them.

Genesis 2:15-18
The Lord God took the man and put him in the Garden of
Eden to work it and take care of it. And the Lord God
commanded the man, "You are free to eat from any tree in
the garden; but you must not eat from the tree of the
knowledge of good and evil, for when you eat from it you
will certainly die."
The Lord God said, "It is not good for the man to be alone. I
will make a helper suitable for him."

 The devil didn't approach Adam directly but he used Eve
who didn't have the full knowledge of what God had said.
Also, he knew Eve had influence over Adam more than
God.
Satan used pride to make them disobey God. He showed
them how they were going to be like God by eating the fruit
of good and evil that God had commanded them not to eat.
That they would have the same wisdom God had therefore
they would not need God again. He turned their hearts away
from God to being self-sufficient. Choosing willingly to eat
the fruit God commanded them not to eat was a declaration
of independence from God.

Genesis 3:1-7
 Now the serpent was more crafty than any of the wild
animals the Lord God had made. He said to the woman,
"Did God really say, 'You must not eat from any tree in the
garden'?"

The woman said to the serpent, "We may eat fruit from the trees in the garden, but God did say, 'You must not eat fruit from the tree that is in the middle of the garden, and you must not touch it, or you will die.'"

"You will not certainly die," the serpent said to the woman. "For God knows that when you eat from it your eyes will be opened, and you will be like God, knowing good and evil."

When the woman saw that the fruit of the tree was good for food and pleasing to the eye, and also desirable for gaining wisdom, she took some and ate it. She also gave some to her husband, who was with her, and he ate it. Then the eyes of both of them were opened, and they realised they were naked; so they sewed fig leaves together and made coverings for themselves.

Obedience to God's word is a sign of dependance on God's grace/strength/help.
This strategy Satan has continued to use it to turn many people against God. God's standard is well defined in his word but Satan will make people find confidence in something else and decree independence from God establishing their own standards. That is the beginning of enmity between God and rebels.

Romans 1:18-32
The wrath of God is being revealed from heaven against all the godlessness and wickedness of people, who suppress the truth by their wickedness, since what may be known about God is plain to them, because God has made it plain to them. For since the creation of the world God's invisible qualities—his eternal power and divine nature—have been clearly seen, being understood from what has been made, so that people are without excuse.

For although they knew God, they neither glorified him as God nor gave thanks to him, but their thinking became futile and their foolish hearts were darkened. Although they claimed to be wise, they became fools and exchanged the glory of the immortal God for images made to look like a mortal human being and birds and animals and reptiles. Therefore God gave them over in the sinful desires of their hearts to sexual impurity for the degrading of their bodies with one another. They exchanged the truth about God for a lie, and worshipped and served created things rather than the Creator—who is forever praised. Amen.

 Because of this, God gave them over to shameful lusts. Even their women exchanged natural sexual relations for unnatural ones.In the same way the men also abandoned natural relations with women and were inflamed with lust for one another. Men committed shameful acts with other men, and received in themselves the due penalty for their error.

Furthermore, just as they did not think it worthwhile to retain the knowledge of God, so God gave them over to a depraved mind, so that they do what ought not to be done. They have become filled with every kind of wickedness, evil, greed and depravity. They are full of envy, murder, strife, deceit and malice. They are gossips, slanderers, God-haters, insolent, arrogant and boastful; they invent ways of doing evil; they disobey their parents; they have no understanding, no fidelity, no love, no mercy. Although they know God's righteous decree that those who do such things deserve death, they not only continue to do these very things but also approve of those who practise them.

2nd corinthians 4:4

The god of this age has blinded the minds of unbelievers, so that they cannot see the light of the gospel that displays the glory of Christ, who is the image of God.

Adam and Eve, like Satan, fell. They were thrown out of the garden of Eden to toil the land. Pride doesn't exalt, it demotes.

Genesis 3:8-24
Then the man and his wife heard the sound of the Lord God as he was walking in the garden in the cool of the day, and they hid from the Lord God among the trees of the garden. But the Lord God called to the man, "Where are you?"
 He answered, "I heard you in the garden, and I was afraid because I was naked; so I hid."
 And he said, "Who told you that you were naked? Have you eaten from the tree that I commanded you not to eat from?"
The man said, "The woman you put here with me—she gave me some fruit from the tree, and I ate it."
 Then the Lord God said to the woman, "What is this you have done?"
The woman said, "The serpent deceived me, and I ate."
So the Lord God said to the serpent, "Because you have done this,

"Cursed are you above all livestock
    and all wild animals!
You will crawl on your belly
    and you will eat dust
    all the days of your life.
 And I will put enmity
    between you and the woman,
    and between your offspring and hers;
he will crush your head,

and you will strike his heel."

To the woman he said,

"I will make your pains in childbearing very severe;
  with painful labour you will give birth to children.
Your desire will be for your husband,
  and he will rule over you."

To Adam he said, "Because you listened to your wife and ate fruit from the tree about which I commanded you, 'You must not eat from it,'

"Cursed is the ground because of you;
  through painful toil you will eat food from it
  all the days of your life.
 It will produce thorns and thistles for you,
  and you will eat the plants of the field.
By the sweat of your brow
  you will eat your food
until you return to the ground,
  since from it you were taken;
for dust you are
  and to dust you will return."

Adam named his wife Eve,because she would become the mother of all the living.
The Lord God made garments of skin for Adam and his wife and clothed them. And the Lord God said, "The man has now become like one of us, knowing good and evil. He must not be allowed to reach out his hand and take also from the tree of life and eat, and live forever." **So the Lord God banished him from the Garden of Eden to work the ground from which he had been taken.** After he drove the

man out, he placed on the east side of the Garden of Eden cherubim and a flaming sword flashing back and forth to guard the way to the tree of life.

CHAPTER THREE: THE TOWER OF BABEL

God had given Adam the instruction that he should fill the earth. The spirit of pride entered people who decided to disobey that command. Their hearts were not in God's desire but to rebel against him.

Genesis 1:28
God blessed them and said to them, "Be fruitful and increase in number; fill the earth and subdue it. Rule over the fish in the sea and the birds in the sky and over every living creature that moves on the ground."

Their confidence was in their ability to build and in their unity brought about by one language,so they decided to use that against God. They decided to build a tower that would reach heaven. See what pride does! it makes you become an enemy of God. When God wanted them to fill the earth, pride directed them to build a tower reaching God.
The results of pride were the same. God came down and confused their one language so that they could not understand each other.
They fell from building the tower to being scattered all over the world.

Genesis 11:1-9
Now the whole world had one language and a common speech. As people moved eastward, they found a plain in Shinar and settled there.

They said to each other, "Come, let's make bricks and bake them thoroughly." They used brick instead of stone, and tar for mortar. **Then they said, "Come, let us build ourselves a city, with a tower that reaches to the heavens, so that we may make a name for ourselves; otherwise we will be scattered over the face of the whole earth."**

But the Lord came down to see the city and the tower the people were building. The Lord said, "If as one people speaking the same language they have begun to do this, then nothing they plan to do will be impossible for them. Come, let us go down and confuse their language so they will not understand each other."

So the Lord scattered them from there over all the earth, and they stopped building the city. That is why it was called Babel—because there the **Lord confused the language of the whole world.** From there the Lord scattered them over the face of the whole earth.

God is all powerful, no one who stands aganist him wins. The devil tried and failed, we have records of such humans that have tried and failed. It's time to humble ourselves and learn so that we don't follow the same path of pride.
Let's set our hearts on God and the force of pride derived from false confidence will not overcome us.

Job 42:2
"I know that you can do all things;
 no purpose of yours can be thwarted.

Romans 15:14
For whatsoever things were written in times past, were written for our learning, that we through patience and comfort of the Scriptures might have hope.

CHAPTER FOUR: KINGS

Nebuchadnezar was a great king that God used to accomplish his purpose on earth. God greatly helped him that he became the greatest king on earth.

Ezekiel 29:19-20
Therefore this is what the Sovereign Lord says: I am going to give Egypt to Nebuchadnezzar, king of Babylon, and he will carry off its wealth. He will loot and plunder the land as pay for his army. I have given him Egypt as a reward for his efforts because he and his army did it for me, declares the Sovereign Lord.

His heart started being moved from God to the great wealth he had acquired. God was merciful and warned him in a vision even gave him time to repent ie bring his heart back from his accomplishments to God. However, Nebuchadnezar was full of pride and he fell so bad to the extent of being driven into the forest to eat grass like animals.
The pattern of pride is the same for nothing is new under the son. The fall is so bad that it leaves an unforgettable mark. Nebuchadnezar decided to humble Himslef and acknowledged God again. He was restored back to his position as king and God restored all. This is our God full of mercy. He knows we are victims of the fallen human nature easily carried away by pride causing us to turn aganist him.

Daniel 4:28-37
All this happened to King Nebuchadnezzar. Twelve months later, **as the king was walking on the roof of the royal palace of Babylon, he said, "Is not this the great Babylon**

I have built as the royal residence, by my mighty power and for the glory of my majesty?"

Even as the words were on his lips, a voice came from heaven, "This is what is decreed for you, King Nebuchadnezzar: Your royal authority has been taken from you. You will be driven away from people and will live with the wild animals; you will eat grass like the ox. Seven times will pass by for you until you acknowledge that the Most High is sovereign over all kingdoms on earth and gives them to anyone he wishes."

Immediately what had been said about Nebuchadnezzar was fulfilled. He was driven away from people and ate grass like an ox. His body was drenched with the dew of heaven until his hair grew like the feathers of an eagle and his nails like the claws of a bird.

At the end of that time, I, Nebuchadnezzar, raised my eyes toward heaven, and my sanity was restored. Then I praised the Most High; I honoured and glorified him who lives forever.

His dominion is an eternal dominion;
　his kingdom endures from generation to generation.
　All the peoples of the earth
　are regarded as nothing.
He does as he pleases
　with the powers of heaven
　and the peoples of the earth.
No one can hold back his hand
　or say to him: "What have you done?"

At the same time that my sanity was restored, my honour and splendour were returned to me for the glory of my kingdom. My advisers and nobles sought me out, and I was restored to my throne and became even

greater than before. *Now I, Nebuchadnezzar, praise and exalt and glorify the King of heaven, because everything he does is right and all his ways are just. And those who walk in pride he is able to humble.*

David, a man after God's heart, was not able to resist this spirit of pride. He saw he was the king, no need to go to battle like other kings. His confidence was no longer in God but in his position as king. When he was not found in his position, he did unthinkable things.
He impregnated another man's wife and even killed the husband. The consequences that fell on David were painful. When he repented however, God restored him by his mercy where he gave him solomon, the king God loved by the same woman she had committed adultery with.

1 Samuel 13:14
 But now thy kingdom shall not continue: the Lord hath sought him a man after his own heart, and the Lord hath commanded him to be captain over his people, because thou hast not kept that which the Lord commanded thee.

Acts 13:22
 And when he had removed him, he raised up unto them David to be their king; to whom also he gave their testimony, and said, I have found David the son of Jesse, a man after mine own heart, which shall fulfil all my will.

2nd samuel 11:1-5
In the spring, at the time when kings go off to war, David sent Joab out with the king's men and the whole Israelite army. They destroyed the Ammonites and besieged Rabbah. But David remained in Jerusalem.

One evening David got up from his bed and walked around on the roof of the palace. From the roof he saw a woman bathing. The woman was very beautiful, and David sent someone to find out about her. The man said, "She is Bathsheba, the daughter of Eliam and **the wife of Uriah the Hittite." Then David sent messengers to get her. She came to him, and he slept with her**. (Now she was purifying herself from her monthly uncleanness.) Then she went back home. **The woman conceived** and sent word to David, saying, "I am pregnant."

2nd samuel 11:14-17
In the morning David wrote a letter to Joab and sent it with Uriah. In it he wrote, "Put Uriah out in front where the fighting is fiercest. Then withdraw from him so he will be struck down and die."
 So while Joab had the city under siege, he put Uriah at a place where he knew the strongest defenders were. When the men of the city came out and fought against Joab, some of the men in David's army fell; moreover, Uriah the Hittite died.

2nd samuel 12:7-14
Then Nathan said to David, "You are the man! This is what the Lord, the God of Israel, says: 'I anointed you king over Israel, and I delivered you from the hand of Saul. I gave your master's house to you, and your master's wives into your arms. I gave you all Israel and Judah. And if all this had been too little, I would have given you even more. **Why did you despise the word of the Lord by doing what is evil in his eyes? You struck down Uriah the Hittite with the sword and took his wife to be your own. You killed him with the sword of the Ammonites. Now, therefore, the sword will never depart from your house,**

because you despised me and took the wife of Uriah the Hittite to be your own.'

"This is what the Lord says: 'Out of your own household I am going to bring calamity on you. Before your very eyes I will take your wives and give them to one who is close to you, and he will sleep with your wives in broad daylight. You did it in secret, but I will do this thing in broad daylight before all Israel.'"

Then David said to Nathan, "I have sinned against the Lord."

Nathan replied, "The Lord has taken away your sin. You are not going to die. But **because by doing this you have shown utter contempt for the Lord, the son born to you will die."**

2nd samuel 24:25
Then David comforted his wife Bathsheba, and he went to her and made love to her. She gave birth to a son, and they named him Solomon. The Lord loved him; and because the Lord loved him, he sent word through Nathan the prophet to name him Jedidiah.

King Uzziah sought God in his days of poverty and God helped him making him so rich. He turned his heart aganist God where he even though he can offer sacrifices to God when God had given that work to priests only.
He died a terrible death.

2nd chronicles 26:1-21
Then all the people of Judah took Uzziah,who was sixteen years old, and made him king in place of his father Amaziah. He was the one who rebuilt Elath and restored it to Judah after Amaziah rested with his ancestors.

Uzziah was sixteen years old when he became king, and he reigned in Jerusalem fifty-two years. His mother's name was Jekoliah; she was from Jerusalem. **He did what was right in the eyes of the Lord, just as his father Amaziah had done. He sought God during the days of Zechariah, who instructed him in the fear of God. As long as he sought the Lord, God gave him success.**

He went to war against the Philistines and broke down the walls of Gath, Jabneh and Ashdod. He then rebuilt towns near Ashdod and elsewhere among the Philistines. **God helped him against the Philistines and against the Arabs who lived in Gur Baal and against the Meunites. The Ammonites brought tribute to Uzziah, and his fame spread as far as the border of Egypt, because he had become very powerful.**

Uzziah built towers in Jerusalem at the Corner Gate, at the Valley Gate and at the angle of the wall, and he fortified them. He also built towers in the wilderness and dug many cisterns, because he had much livestock in the foothills and in the plain. He had people working his fields and vineyards in the hills and in the fertile lands, for he loved the soil.

Uzziah had a well-trained army, ready to go out by divisions according to their numbers as mustered by Jeiel the secretary and Maaseiah the officer under the direction of Hananiah, one of the royal officials. The total number of family leaders over the fighting men was 2,600. 13 Under their command was an army of 307,500 men trained for war, a powerful force to support the king against his enemies. Uzziah provided shields, spears, helmets, coats of armour, bows and slingstones for the entire army. In Jerusalem he made devices invented for use on the towers and on the corner defences so that soldiers could shoot arrows and hurl large stones from the walls. **His fame spread far and wide, for he was greatly helped until he became powerful.**

But after Uzziah became powerful, his pride led to his downfall. He was unfaithful to the Lord his God, and entered the temple of the Lord to burn incense on the altar of incense. Azariah the priest with eighty other courageous priests of the Lord followed him in. They confronted King Uzziah and said, "It is not right for you, Uzziah, to burn incense to the Lord. That is for the priests, the descendants of Aaron, who have been consecrated to burn incense. Leave the sanctuary, for you have been unfaithful; and you will not be honoured by the Lord God."

Uzziah, who had a censer in his hand ready to burn incense, became angry. While he was raging at the priests in their presence before the incense altar in the Lord's temple, leprosy broke out on his forehead. When Azariah the chief priest and all the other priests looked at him, they saw that **he had leprosy on his forehead, so they hurried him out. Indeed, he himself was eager to leave, because the Lord had afflicted him.**

King Uzziah had leprosy until the day he died. He lived in a separate house leprous, and banned from the temple of the Lord. Jotham his son had charge of the palace and governed the people of the land.

Many start well but finish very bad. They start in humilty where there hearts are fully on God until they get what they have always desired. Money, job, marriage partner, power, postion etc and these things turn their hearts away from God.

Check your heart to ensure it remains on God despite the victories he will help you achieve. Never let them distract you from the main person for all things pass away but God remains.

Galatians 5:7-10

You were running a good race. Who cut in on you to keep you from obeying the truth? That kind of persuasion does not come from the one who calls you. "A little yeast works through the whole batch of dough." I am confident in the Lord that you will take no other view. The one who is throwing you into confusion, whoever that may be, will have to pay the penalty.

2nd Corinthians 13:5
Examine yourselves, to see whether you are in the faith. Test yourselves. Or do you not realise this about yourselves, that Jesus Christ is in you?—unless indeed you fail to meet the test!

CHAPTER FIVE: JESUS
God showed us the pattern of lifting which is humility i.e. total dependance on God.

Proverbs 3:5-6
Trust in the Lord with all your heart
  and lean not on your own understanding;
 in all your ways submit to him,
  and he will make your paths straight.

Jesus was in the class of God. However, he became a human and even died on the cross for sins he didn't commit. He humbled himself so much in obedience to God's will and this made God lift him to the highest position.

Philippians 2:5-11
In your relationships with one another, have the same mindset as Christ Jesus:
Who, **being in very nature God,**

**did not consider equality with God something to be
used to his own advantage;**
 rather, he made himself nothing
 by taking the very nature of a servant,
 being made in human likeness.
 And being found in appearance as a man,
 he humbled himself
 by becoming obedient to death—
 even death on a cross!
 Therefore God exalted him to the highest place
 and gave him the name that is above every name,
that at the name of Jesus every knee should bow,
 in heaven and on earth and under the earth,
 and every tongue acknowledge that Jesus Christ is Lord,
 to the glory of God the Father.

 He got the seat Satan so desired to get but the way was
different. When Satan chose to disobey God and fell, Jesus
obeyed God and was exalted to sitting at the right hand of
God.

Ephesians 1:20-23
That power is the same as the mighty strength he exerted
when he raised Christ from the dead and seated him at his
right hand in the heavenly realms, far above all rule and
authority, power and dominion, and every name that is
invoked, not only in the present age but also in the one to
come. And God placed all things under his feet and
appointed him to be head over everything for the church,
which is his body, the fullness of him who fills everything in
every way.

To go high you must go down first. It's a choice to die daily and keep the heart focused on God despite the many things calling for our attention in the world.

Everytime we obey the commands of God we are showing our dependance on God and that is humility attracting more Grace for exaltation.

Ephesians 4:7-10

But to each one of us grace has been given as Christ apportioned it. This is why it says:

"When he ascended on high,
    he took many captives
    and gave gifts to his people."

(What does "he ascended" mean except that he also descended to the lower, earthly regions? He who descended is the very one who ascended higher than all the heavens, in order to fill the whole universe.

Proverbs 22:4

Humility is the fear of the Lord;
    its wages are riches and honour and life.

1st corinthians 15:31

declare by my rejoicing in you which I have in Christ Jesus our Lord: I die daily.

CONCLUSION

May you be totally surrendered to God that your heart derives it's confidence in him.

God is a tester, he will not trust until he proves where your heart is.

Psalms 139:23-24
Search me, God, and know my heart;
 test me and know my anxious thoughts.
See if there is any offensive way in me,
 and lead me in the way everlasting.

Abraham needed a child so much that when God gave him what he needed, he asked him for the same child.

Genesis 15:1-4
After this, the word of the Lord came to Abram in a vision:

"Do not be afraid, Abram.
 I am your shield,
 your very great reward."

But Abram said, "Sovereign Lord, what can you give me since I remain childless and the one who will inherit my estate is Eliezer of Damascus?" And Abram said, "You have given me no children; so a servant in my household will be my heir."
 Then the word of the Lord came to him: "This man will not be your heir, but a son who is your own flesh and blood will be your heir."

The good thing with Abraham was that he had put his trust fully in God and not in his son. He was willing to let the son go to prove his obedience to God.
This made God vow to bless Abraham and give him nations.

Genesis 22:1-19
Some time later God tested Abraham. He said to him, "Abraham!"

"Here I am," he replied.

Then God said, "Take your son, your only son, whom you love—Isaac—and go to the region of Moriah. Sacrifice him there as a burnt offering on a mountain I will show you."

Early the next morning Abraham got up and loaded his donkey. He took with him two of his servants and his son Isaac. When he had cut enough wood for the burnt offering, he set out for the place God had told him about. On the third day Abraham looked up and saw the place in the distance. He said to his servants, "Stay here with the donkey while I and the boy go over there. We will worship and then we will come back to you."

Abraham took the wood for the burnt offering and placed it on his son Isaac, and he himself carried the fire and the knife. As the two of them went on together, Isaac spoke up and said to his father Abraham, "Father?"

"Yes, my son?" Abraham replied.

"The fire and wood are here," Isaac said, "but where is the lamb for the burnt offering?"

Abraham answered, "God himself will provide the lamb for the burnt offering, my son." And the two of them went on together.

When they reached the place God had told him about, Abraham built an altar there and arranged the wood on it. He bound his son Isaac and laid him on the altar, on top of the wood. Then he reached out his hand and took the knife to slay his son. But the angel of the Lord called out to him from heaven, "Abraham! Abraham!"

"Here I am," he replied.

"Do not lay a hand on the boy," he said. **"Do not do anything to him. Now I know that you fear God, because you have not withheld from me your son, your only son."** Abraham looked up and there in a thicket he saw a ram caught by its horns. He went over and took the ram and sacrificed it as a burnt offering instead of his son. So Abraham called that place The Lord Will Provide. And to this day it is said, "On the mountain of the Lord it will be provided."

The angel of the Lord called to Abraham from heaven a second time and said, "I swear by myself, declares the Lord, that because you have done this and have not withheld your son, your only son, I will surely bless you and make your descendants as numerous as the stars in the sky and as the sand on the seashore. Your descendants will take possession of the cities of their enemies, and through your offspring all nations on earth will be blessed, because you have obeyed me."

Then Abraham returned to his servants, and they set off together for Beersheba. And Abraham stayed in Beersheba.

Anything satan shows you that it's greater than God will just limit you to access the abundance God has.
If Abraham held on to his son he would not be the father of nations today.

Psalms 78:41
Yea, they turned back and tested God, and limited the Holy One of Israel.

Solomon's heart was fully on God when he began. God enabled him to rise to an extent of being the richest king in his time.

1st kings 3:2-14

The people, however, were still sacrificing at the high places, because a temple had not yet been built for the Name of the Lord. **Solomon showed his love for the Lord by walking according to the instructions given him by his father David,** except that he offered sacrifices and burned incense on the high places.

The king went to Gibeon to offer sacrifices, for that was the most important high place, and **Solomon offered a thousand burnt offerings on that altar. At Gibeon the Lord appeared to Solomon during the night in a dream, and God said, "Ask for whatever you want me to give you."**

Solomon answered, "You have shown great kindness to your servant, my father David, because he was faithful to you and righteous and upright in heart. You have continued this great kindness to him and have given him a son to sit on his throne this very day.

"Now, Lord my God, you have made your servant king in place of my father David. But I am only a little child and do not know how to carry out my duties. Your servant is here among the people you have chosen, a great people, too numerous to count or number. So **give your servant a discerning heart to govern your people and to distinguish between right and wrong**. For who is able to govern this great people of yours?"

The Lord was pleased that Solomon had asked for this. So God said to him, "Since you have asked for this and not for long life or wealth for yourself, nor have asked for the death of your enemies but for discernment in administering justice, I will do what you have asked. I will give you a wise and discerning heart, so that there will never have been anyone like you, nor will there ever be. Moreover, **I will give you what you have not asked for—both wealth and honour—so that in your lifetime you will have no equal among kings**. And if you walk in obedience to me and keep my decrees and commands as David your father did, I will give you a long life."

2nd chronicles 9:13-28

Every year King Solomon received over twenty-five tons of gold, in addition to the taxes paid by the traders and merchants. The kings of Arabia and the governors of the Israelite districts also brought him silver and gold. Solomon made two hundred large shields, each of which was covered with about fifteen pounds of beaten gold, and three hundred smaller shields, each covered with about eight pounds of beaten gold. He had them all placed in the Hall of the Forest of Lebanon.

The king also had a large throne made. Part of it was covered with ivory and the rest of it was covered with pure gold. Six steps led up to the throne, and there was a footstool attached to it, covered with gold. There were arms on each side of the throne, and the figure of a lion stood at each side. Twelve figures of lions were on the steps, one at either end of each step. No throne like this had ever existed in any other kingdom.

All of King Solomon's drinking cups were made of gold, and all the utensils in the Hall of the Forest of Lebanon were of pure gold. Silver was not considered valuable in Solomon's day. He had a fleet of ocean-going ships sailing with King Hiram's fleet. Every three years his fleet would return, bringing gold, silver, ivory, apes, and monkeys.

King Solomon was richer and wiser than any other king in the world. They all consulted him, to hear the wisdom that God had given him. Each of them brought Solomon gifts—articles of silver and gold, robes, weapons, spices, horses, and mules. This continued year after year.

King Solomon also had four thousand stalls for his chariots and horses, and had twelve thousand cavalry horses. Some of them he kept in Jerusalem and the rest he stationed in various other cities. He was supreme ruler of all the kings in the territory from the Euphrates River to Philistia and the Egyptian border. During his reign silver was as common in Jerusalem as stone, and cedar was as plentiful as ordinary sycamore in the foothills of Judah. Solomon imported horses from Musri and from every other country.

His heart was moved from God to his great name and wealth that he disobeyed God. He became his own god. He married the women from the nations God had said Israel should not marry from, he built altars for their gods and even offered sacrifices to them. Wealth has such power that even if God had appeared to Solomon twice, that didn't stop his heart from turning away.

1st kings 11:1-13

King Solomon, however, loved many foreign women besides Pharaoh's daughter—Moabites, Ammonites, Edomites, Sidonians and Hittites. They were from nations about which the Lord had told the Israelites, "You must not intermarry with them, because they will surely turn your hearts after their gods." Nevertheless, Solomon held fast to them in love. He had seven hundred wives of royal birth and three hundred concubines, and his wives led him astray. **As Solomon grew old, his wives**

turned his heart after other gods, and his heart was not fully devoted to the Lord his God, as the heart of David his father had been. He followed Ashtoreth the goddess of the Sidonians, and Molek the detestable god of the Ammonites. So Solomon did evil in the eyes of the Lord; he did not follow the Lord completely, as David his father had done.

On a hill east of Jerusalem, **Solomon built a high place for Chemosh the detestable god of Moab, and for Molek the detestable god of the Ammonites. He did the same for all his foreign wives, who burned incense and offered sacrifices to their gods.**

The Lord became angry with Solomon because his heart had turned away from the Lord, the God of Israel, who had appeared to him twice. Although he had forbidden Solomon to follow other gods, Solomon did not keep the Lord's command. So the Lord said to Solomon, "Since this is your attitude and you have not kept my covenant and my decrees, which I commanded you, I will most certainly tear the kingdom away from you and give it to one of your subordinates. Nevertheless, for the sake of David your father, I will not do it during your lifetime. I will tear it out of the hand of your son. Yet I will not tear the whole kingdom from him, but will give him one tribe for the sake of David my servant and for the sake of Jerusalem, which I have chosen."

He fell so bad that he saw life to be meaningless. Nothing satisfied his heart and he discovered in the last days of his life that obedience to God is the only meaning a human has in life.

Ecclesiastes 1:2
The words of the Teacher, son of David, king in Jerusalem:

"Meaningless! Meaningless!"
    says the Teacher.
"Utterly meaningless!
    Everything is meaningless."

Ecclesiastes 12:13-14
Let us hear the conclusion of the whole matter: **Fear God, and keep his commandments: for this is the whole duty of man.**
For God shall bring every work into judgement, with every secret thing, whether it be good, or whether it be evil.

God created all things and as long as they remain connected to their source they live. People were made from God's image, anything that can take away the heart of a human from God is a distractor. That person will fall and find no meaning in all the things they gather.
Stay connected to God who is your source and you will live. You will be like a tree ever green but when you let satan move your heart away from God you will wither.

Psalms 1:1-4
Blessed is the one
    who does not walk in step with the wicked
or stand in the way that sinners take
    or sit in the company of mockers,
 but whose delight is in the law of the Lord,
    and who meditates on his law day and night.
 That person is like a tree planted by streams of water,
    which yields its fruit in season
and whose leaf does not wither—
    whatever they do prospers.

Not so the wicked!
   They are like chaff
   that the wind blows away.

It's your responsibility to check yourself and see if you are still in faith. If things or people are moving you away from God, repent ie turn back to God's ways.

Jeremiah 6:16
Thus says the Lord: Stand by the roads and look; and ask for the eternal paths, where the good, old way is; then walk in it, and you will find rest for your souls. But they said, We will not walk in it!

May the Lord grant that which is the desire of your heart. When he does, ensure you don't let it take your heart away from God. Worship the Lord your God only, don't idolise money, people, knowledge, power, gifts etc. Remember all these are gifts from God who is the source. Stay connected to the source and you will have more and more grace to move you from glory to glory.

Psalms 37:4
Delight yourself in the Lord,
   and he will give you the desires of your heart.

James 1:17
Every good and perfect gift is from above, coming down from the Father of the heavenly lights, who does not change like shifting shadows.

Understand also the reason God gives you all these gifts is to support the gospel of Christ so that many can get to know God.

Psalms 35:27-28
Let them shout for joy, and be glad, that favour my righteous cause: yea, let them say continually, Let the Lord be magnified, which hath pleasure in the prosperity of his servant

Also, so that you can be a blessing to people in need. God loves people and it's because of people he came to die. You can be God's vessel to show that love physically as you enjoy life.

Genesis 12:2
I will make you into a great nation,
    and I will bless you;
I will make your name great,
    and **you will be a blessing.**

1st Timothy 6:17 19
Command those who are rich in this present world not to be arrogant nor to put their hope in wealth, which is so uncertain, but to put their hope in God, who richly provides us with everything for our enjoyment. Command them to do good, to be rich in good deeds, and to be generous and willing to share.In this way they will lay up treasure for themselves as a firm foundation for the coming age, so that they may take hold of the life that is truly life.

JOHN 13:17

NOW THAT YOU KNOW THESE THINGS, YOU WILL BE BLESSED IF YOU DO THEM.

More Grace on you as keep your heart established on God.

If you need help to study God's word, please email me at pstmaryjoy@gmail.com and I will guide you through.

To get my other books in amazon, click this link https://www.amazon.com/author/marynyandia